Index to
AMERICAN SHORT STORY AWARD COLLECTIONS 1970–90

Index to
AMERICAN
SHORT STORY
AWARD COLLECTIONS
1970–90

Thomas E. Kennedy

Pushcart Prize
American Fiction Series
AWP Short Fiction Award
Drue Heinz Literature Prize
Flannery O'Connor Award
University of Illinois Short Fiction Series
Iowa School of Letters Award

PS
374
.55
K46x
1993
West Ref

G.K. Hall & Co.
An Imprint of Macmillan Publishing Company
New York

Maxwell Macmillan Canada
Toronto

Maxwell Macmillan International
New York • Oxford • Singapore • Sydney

G.K. Hall & Co.
An Imprint of Macmillan Publishing Company
866 Third Avenue
New York, NY 10022

Maxwell Macmillan Canada, Inc.
1200 Eglinton Avenue East
Suite 200
Don Mills, Ontario M3C 3N1

Macmillan Publishing Company is part of the Maxwell Communication Group of Companies.

Library of Congress Catalog Card Number: 92-38295

Printed in the United States of America

Printing number
1 2 3 4 5 6 7 8 9 10

Library of Congress Cataloging-in-Publication Data

Kennedy, Thomas E.
    Index to American short story award collections, 1970-90 / Thomas E. Kennedy
        p. cm.
    Includes bibliographical references and index.
    ISBN 0-8161-1819-1
    1. Short stories, American—Bibliography. 2. Literary prizes—United States—
Indexes. 3. Short stories, American—Indexes.
I. Title.
Z1231.F4k46 1993
[PS374.S5]
016.813'0108054—dc20   92-38295
                                                            CIP

For the short story people:
the ones who write them
the ones who publish them
and most of all
the ones who read them.

CONTENTS

II. SERIES OF SINGLE-AUTHOR COLLECTIONS

ABOUT THE AUTHOR

Thomas E. Kennedy's other books include a novel, *Crossing Borders* (Watermark Press, 1990), and three books of literary criticism: *Robert Coover: A Study of the Short Fiction* (Macmillan, 1992); *The American Short Story Today* (United States Information Service/Danish Association for American Studies, 1991); and *Andre Dubus: A Study of the Short Fiction* (Twayne, 1988). His short stories, essays, interviews, reviews, poems, and translations have appeared in more than a hundred literary journals and anthologies in the United States and Europe and have been translated into Danish and Serbo-Croatian.

Kennedy holds a B.A. (summa cum laude) from Fordham University, an M.F.A. from Vermont College of Norwich University, and a Ph.D. from Copenhagen University. He has taught creative writing at the Vermont College M.F.A. Program, the Emerson College International Writing Seminar in the Netherlands, the Women's Institute for Continuing Education in Paris, and the University of Maryland in Copenhagen.

Since the mid-1970s he has lived in Denmark with his wife and two children where he serves, inter alia, as European Editor of *Cimarron Review*. His fiction has earned a *Pushcart Prize*, Charles Angoff Award, *Passages North/NEA* Emerging Writer recognition, and a three-year Theodore B. Goodman Grant from the City College of New York.

ACKNOWLEDGMENTS

The author would like to express deep and sincere thanks to the following for their generous advice, cooperation, and assistance:

David Major, Oklahoma State University
Bill Henderson, Pushcart Press
Charles East, University of Georgia Press
Paul Zimmer, University of Iowa Press
Michael C. White, American Fiction
Ann Lowry Weir, University of Illinois Press
Ed Ochester, University of Pittsburgh Press
Associated Writing Programs

PREFACE

An American National Treasure

Probably every country has hidden cultural treasures—the illuminated manuscripts of Ireland and the psalms and folk ballads of Denmark, for example. In America we can confidently point to short stories as our hidden treasure. I do not refer primarily to the celebrated stories of writers such as Poe, Hawthorne, Irving, Melville, Twain, Crane, London, Anderson, Hemingway, Fitzgerald, Faulkner, Steinbeck, but to those of the thousands upon thousands of dedicated craftsmen who over the past couple of centuries have devoted themselves to creating new examples of the marvelous short story form, using it as an instrument of coming to terms with the mystery of our lives, as a way to complete the insufficiency of our existential ignorance, as a means to entertain, delight, enlighten, and enrich.

From the beginning, the magazine has played an important role in the literary history of the United States. In the first years of the American colonies, while facilities for book publication were scarce, magazines were widespread. All of the great early American short story writers published their work originally in magazines, as have most of their successors since. Even Edgar Allan Poe's famous theoretical formulation of the genre made its first appearance on the pages of a magazine in the form of a book review of Hawthorne's *Twice-Told Tales.*

The American colonies' first magazine debuted in the mid-eighteenth century. It is estimated that by 1800 between 400 and 500 short stories had been published in American magazines. By 1820, more than a hundred magazines, carrying many hundreds of short stories, had already appeared and disappeared.

As Eugene Current Garcia points out in his study *The American Short Story before 1850* (Twayne, 1983):

> The magazinist during these transitional decades provided probably the only feasible means of producing a new national literature since he alone possessed the business methods and manufacturing techniques needed.

Magazines continued to play an important role in the history of the American short story right up to the present century. Mass circulation magazines like the *Saturday Evening Post* were major promoters of the short stories of writers like Hemingway, Faulkner, and Fitzgerald. *The New Yorker*, too, has nurtured many a literary reputation of writers as varied as John Updike, Truman Capote, J. D. Salinger, and Donald Barthelme.

In recent years, the commercial magazine market for the short story has dwindled considerably. But, at the same time, literary magazines have thrived and multiplied, and there are several thousand in publication today. These small literary journals have long been the mainstay of the American short story. Periodicals like Whit Burnett's *Story Magazine*, George Plimpton's *The Paris Review*, and a host of others are legendary in their support and promotion of the genre and its practitioners.

These magazines have given new writers, middle-career writers, and many of the prominent, established writers, too, a place to publish their best work without its being squeezed between slick advertisements in magazines whose aim is to make money, their editors altering stories, often without permission, for no reason other than to fit them into the remaining space or to avoid offending a sponsor. (Andre Dubus, for example, tells how *Penthouse* magazine made scores of unauthorized changes in one of his stories. The *New Yorker*, too, makes changes, but not without first securing the author's agreement.)

Trying to estimate the number of short stories published every year in the United States is something like trying to guess the number of jelly beans in a jar. There are obviously many, but how many? If, say, 2,000 quarterlies each publish four short stories per issue (some publish fewer, but many publish more), that would constitute 32,000 new short stories annually, which is probably a conservative estimate. Considering that approximately one percent of the stories submitted to the little magazines are accepted for publication, most of them have, therefore, survived a rather stringent process of selection, making them at the least not too bad, a good many pretty good, and more than a few excellent.

If you're interested in short stories, if you *love* short stories, you must realize that most literary magazines have a small circulation. An issue appears, is distributed in 300 to perhaps 5,000 copies, and then slips away, leaving barely a ripple. Of these many thousands, a few stories are selected for reprint in the annual *Best American Short Stories* (Houghton Mifflin) and *O. Henry* (Doubleday) award volumes, a total of perhaps forty stories each year. In addition, perhaps a hundred other stories are noted in the back of the *Best American* stories volume for distinction.

What happens to the others? How is one to learn about them? Get hold of them? If you love short stories, how do you find more than the few handfuls honored by *Best* and *O. Henry* (and documented in Ray Lewis White's *An Index to Best American Short Stories and O. Henry Awards* published by G. K. Hall, 1988)? How can literary researchers, scholars, students, and the general reader explore the vast sea of stories published each year?

Best and *O. Henry* represent only a part of the selection process. A large number of other series provide access to many of the fine stories published each year in award volumes. The purpose of this book is to provide a central index from which short story lovers, researchers, students, and teachers may gain an overview of some of the more outstanding of these series.

This index covers seven such series, the oldest of which began in 1970, the most recent in 1987. Two of the series are anthologies of individual stories by a range of authors, while the other five represent series of single-author collections. Other fine series also exist— the University of Missouri Breakthrough Series, the Milkweed National Fiction Award, the Triquarterly award series, the collections published by Louisiana State University Press, Iowa's John Simmons Short Fiction Award, the Illinois State University/Fiction-

Collective-Two National Fiction Competition, and Morty Sklar's Editors' Choice series from the Spirit That Moves Us Press in Jackson Heights, New York—but these either appear irregularly, are very new, do not appear as actual series, or are mixed competitions not focused exclusively on short fiction. The seven series in this book constitute the most representative harvest of the past two decades. They all draw first and foremost upon the wealth of literary quarterlies published in the United States today, taking into consideration not only the well-known, well-established, well-funded journals, but also the smaller, newer ones that operate hand-to-mouth. It cannot be too strongly or too frequently emphasized that the American literary journals—both the university journals and the independent ones—serve as the sanctuary of the short story; without them, short fiction writers would find themselves in a disheartening situation.

Those interested in further information on today's literary journals are referred to the *Directory of Literary Magazines* (Council of Literary Magazines and Presses, New York City), Len Fulton's *International Directory of Little Magazines and Small Presses* (Dustbooks, P. O. Box 100, Paradise, California 95969), the *MLA Directory of Periodicals* (Modern Language Association, 10 Astor Place, New York, New York 10003), and *The American Short Story Today* (DAAS/USIS, Fragariavej 12, DK-2900 Hellerup, Denmark). For more information about the state of the literary magazine, the reader should investigate the periodical *Poets and Writers* and the newsletter of the Council of Literary Magazines and Small Presses, both in New York City, and the *AWP Chronicle* at Old Dominion University, Norfolk, Virginia.

Although, technically, this index spans only twenty years, the stories published in the collections and anthologies reach back as far as five decades. A short story collection, particularly one enshrined in such an award volume, will frequently represent many years of a writer's best work. While the award is dated with a single year, it nevertheless may reflect the best effort of an entire career as well as the endeavors of scores of literary journal editors to select and present outstanding examples of the stories that come their way.

These seven series are little more than the tip of the iceberg. As the short stories of America represent one of our richest national treasures, it is heartening to note how little this treasure has to do with money—the stories are written, published, distributed, and read beyond the frame of commerce. They are works of art in the best sense of the term, solid evidence of the rich culture beneath the superficiality that unfortunately characterizes so much of American life today.

These series and the small press in general often stand as a sanctuary for free expression in an America of the nineties where even the fairy tales of Hans Christian Andersen have been subjected to the censor's judgment. It is difficult to believe that a publisher, under the banner of political correctness, could presume to tamper with international literary treasures, attempting to turn Andersen's beautiful, magical realism into sentimental pap.

Censorship is a thing born politically and commercially for common reasons: the fear of offending the mass and conventional presumptions that pass as "standards" in our society. Because it might cost them their jobs, U.S. politicians fear offending fundamentalist religious stands concerning abortion, sexual freedom, and "obscenity." For the same reason, many academic writers, editors, and even university presses fear confounding *politically correct* presumptions or placing themselves in a position of being brandable as "racist" or "sexist," words that carry an emotional charge similar to that of the word "communist" in the fifties. Commercial publishers fear offending anyone who may have an influence on the mass market—their concern is not with offending "good taste," but rather the willingness to buy. This censorship has grown worse by the year through the eighties and continues to intensify. Recent years have witnessed the oubreak of threats to the first amendment guarantees of the constitution from sources as unlikely as the National Endowment for the Arts, under pressure from opportunistic politicians.

For these reasons, the small press in the United States is of vital importance to the promotion of freedom of expression and for making a place for the literary art of people unwilling to subject themselves to political, academic, or commercial pressure. Most of the series do not take this cause as a crusade (although some, like the *Pushcart*, do); many of the stories that appear in today's literary journals are probably at least to some extent shaped by the fear of offending. Moreover, many university presses include in their reasons for rejecting manuscripts judgments of "sexism," "racism," and even "blasphemy" that have little or nothing to do with the real sexist and racist issues troubling society. But the small presses and especially series like the *Pushcart* hold open a place for writers whose visions do not fit the "standard," which is a vital function.

Preface

Twenty years ago, the question of censorship seemed long behind us in the United States. An enlightened American Supreme Court had secured the right of Americans to read controversial works by James Joyce, Henry Miller, and other fine writers previously denied to them. Who would think that such battles would have to be fought again in the nineties? The small press can serve as a powerful force in support of writers under the pressure of betraying that which they perceive as truth.

For these reasons, I felt it fitting to index the information contained in this volume, to centralize and make it more readily available to readers, researchers, teachers, and students—and to honor the efforts of the fine writers, editors, and publishers involved.

Thomas E. Kennedy
Copenhagen

I. ANTHOLOGIES

The Pushcart Prize, Best of the Small Presses, 1976–90
The American Fiction Series, 1987–90

The Pushcart Prize, Best of the Small Presses, 1976–90

How does one survey the literature of an entire nation, especially a nation as large and diverse as the United States? Can one ever hope to know what is happening at the moment in American letters? Or *where* it is happening? How are relevant publishing decisions made?

Chances are the big decisions, the visible ones, are made by commerce. A colleague of mine who sold her first novel to Simon & Schuster not long ago, on a two-book contract with a $20,000 advance, grew disillusioned by the production process. Her editor was a stern taskmaster in making her revise the novel. They argued and fought, and, when she tried to defend a section of the book on the grounds of artistic soundness, her editor replied, "We are not talking about art at the moment; we are readying your book for the market."

In the market, the almighty dollar is king. There is nothing wrong with a writer's having literary merit as long as said writer sells books and earns money for his or her publisher. But where decisions have to be made between literary merit and earning power, the latter virtue more often than not is decisive.

The *Pushcart Prize* anthology is for those readers who wish to explore the free field of American writing, where people write for the sake of writing, "making no compromise with public taste," as *Paris Review* editor George Plimpton notes in the introduction to *The Pushcart Prize, X*. The series rewards writers who disregard the commercial demands of the editors of large commercial publishing houses, demands that editors make because it is important for their editorial careers that "their" books not fail commercially.

It sounds like a joke. A pushcart is a street peddler's wagon. But the little magazines and small presses of the United States might be thought of as representing street peddlers when compared to large, sleek, commercial ventures. And the Pushcart series, in its nearly two decades, has done honor to the more than 2,000 little magazines and small presses throughout the United States.

Each year, the *Pushcart Prize* editors select and reprint some 500 pages of poetry and prose that they believe represent the most significant among the tens of thousands of pages published annually by small presses and literary journals. Each *Pushcart* volume includes a comprehensive index of the work that has appeared in the series to date. If we look at the index of volume XVI/1991–92, we will see that the first sixteen books of the series have reprinted 289 short stories, 473 poems, and 138 pieces of nonfiction and paid homage to many hundreds of others in the supplementary select list of outstanding writers and publishers that appears in the back of each volume.

But the *Pushcart* volume is not merely another anthology like the *Best American Short Stories* and the *O. Henry Award* annuals, two better-known, noteworthy American literary events. Significant differences distinguish the *Pushcart* and make it considerably more representative of the literary life of the year. The stories that appear in the 75-year-old *O. Henry* volume are selected by a single editor (since 1965, William Abrahams), those of the 70-yearold *Best* by two editors (Shannon Ravenel, in cooperation with a prominent guest editor chosen for each year). The *Pushcart* selections are taken from the several thousand nominations made annually by small presses, periodicals, and the more than 200 members of the editorial board, headed by the series founder and publisher, Bill Henderson.

Once a writer is selected for inclusion in the series, that writer is also nominated to join the list of contributing editors and to serve as a kind of talent scout, nominating others to appear in the series. Thus, the *Pushcart Prize* is the closest thing in the American literary scene to peer review. While Bill Henderson was and is the prime mover of the series, the roster of founding editors makes clear that its creation was not the act of a person working in isolation; he had the support of others who shared his concern about the state of publishing in the United States—writers such as Anaïs Nin, Buckminster Fuller, Charles Newman, Gordon Lish, Joyce Carol Oates, Ishmael Reed, Leslie Fiedler, Paul Bowles, and Ralph Ellison.

Looking down the list of sources from which the stories in the *Best* and *O. Henry* volumes have been harvested, one finds a preponderance of commercial periodicals—*The Atlantic, New Yorker, Harper's, Esquire*, and *Playboy*—and of the older, more institutionalized literary journals. Pointing this out is not intended to denigrate the quality of the stories, which are generally excellent, but to suggest that a certain element of elitism may be at play in those volumes. A story in the *New Yorker* has a running start toward appreciation—the reader *expects* it to be good and knows that it has been purchased for several thousand dollars instead of the fifty to two hundred or even less paid by little magazines.

By contrast, the selections in the *Pushcart Prize* volume can only be made from small presses and small magazine publishers; large commercial sources are excluded. Bill Henderson started publishing the *Pushcart Prize* volumes, as he stated in the first volume of the *The Pushcart Prize* (1976), as a reaction to "a culture too often dominated by big bucks conglomerates" and in order to accord "recognition to those authors and editors who for too long have labored in anonymity." While predominantly American, the *Pushcart* is also open to nominations from small international presses and has featured a number of works in translation.

If we look down the list of names of writers who have appeared in the *Pushcart Prize*, we find a range that spans the unknown, slightly known, and the famous. If we look at the earliest volumes, we will find names that have since become prominent—Paul Auster, Margaret Atwood, Jane Bowles, Paul Bowles, Andre Dubus, John Irving, Italo Calvino, Joyce Carol Oates, Raymond Carver, Anne Tyler, Cynthia Ozick. But most of the names are unknown, or on their way to earning greater renown. Unheralded works, even debut pieces by new writers, exist side by side with those by Nobel laureates (the first volume, for example, includes pieces by Saul Bellow and Octavio Paz alongside a poem by Michael Hogan, a prisoner in the maximum security ward of the Arizona State Prison). Further, no single style is maintained throughout the series. The *Pushcart* volumes include realists, surrealists, postmodernists, stories, poems, and essays in most conceivable forms. The 1990–91 volume, for example, includes twenty-eight stories, twenty-six poems, and four essays (clearly the series favors the short story form over others). Special mention is made of an additional 126 stories, fifteen essays, and 105 poems—a guide to further reading for the profoundly interested reader (though to obtain those additional works it would be necessary for the reader to purchase about 250 different magazines at a cost of several hundred dollars, plus postage; by contrast, the *Pushcart* volumes sell for about $28 apiece in hardback, $15 in paper).

Each volume in the series (since volume VII) begins with an introduction by a writer with a special background in the small press. The first seven volumes were introduced by series editor Bill Henderson, the later volumes by significant small press literary figures such as George Plimpton, Cynthia Ozick, Tess Gallagher, and Russell Banks.

The *Pushcart Prize* is a series for those who wish to look beneath the surface of the commercial literary market in the United States, an anthology for those interested in a continuing selection of many of the finest stories appearing in the American small presses. Anyone in love with the short story form will find great pleasure in the *Pushcart*.

CHRONOLOGICAL INDEX WITH STORY CONTENTS

The Pushcart Prize, Best of the Small Presses (1976–77 Edition). Edited by Bill Henderson with the Pushcart Prize Editors, introduction by Bill Henderson. Wainscott, NY: The Pushcart Press, 1976, cloth; New York: Avon, 1976, pb, 438 pp.

Short fiction contents:

Kranes, David, "Cordials" (from *Triquarterly*), 3–9
Tyler, Anne, "The Artificial Family" (from *Southern Review*), ll–18
Francis, H.E., "A Chronicle of Love" (from *Kansas Quarterly*), 31–48
Carver, Raymond, "So Much Water So Close to Home" (from *Spectrum*), 50–68
Gass, William, "I Wish You Wouldn't" (from *Partisan Review*), 98–114
Reyzen, Avrom, "The Dog" (from *Antaeus*), 115–21

The Pushcart Prize II: Best of the Small Presses (1977–78 Edition). Edited by Bill Henderson with the Pushcart Prize Editors, introduction by Bill Henderson. Wainscott, NY: The Pushcart Press, 1977, cloth; New York: Avon, 1977, pb, 527 pp.

Short fiction contents:

The Pushcart Prize, III: Best of the Small Presses (1978–79 Edition). Edited by Bill Henderson with the Pushcart Prize Editors, introduction by Bill Henderson. Wainscott, NY: The Pushcart Press, 1978, cloth; New York: Avon, 1978, pb, 543 pp.

Short fiction contents:

The Pushcart Prize, IV: Best of the Small Presses (1979–80 Edition). Edited by Bill Henderson with the Pushcart Prize Editors, introduction by Bill Henderson. Wainscott, NY: The Pushcart Press, 1979, cloth; New York: Avon, 1979, pb, 591 pp.

Short fiction contents:

Wiebe, Dallas, "Night Flight to Stockholm" (from *Paris Review*), 133–41

Taggart, Shirly Ann, "Ghosts Like Them" (from *Hudson Review*), 161–75

Weinstein, Jeff, "A Jean-Marie Cookbook" (from *Sun and Moon*), 185–222

Schott, Max, "Early Winter" (from *Massachusetts Review*), 239–66

Hall, James B., "My Work in California" (from *Missouri Review*), 267–83

Smiley, Jane, "Jeffrey, Believe Me" (from *Triquarterly*), 299–305

Porter, Joe Ashby, "Sweetness, A Thinking Machine" (from *Sun and Moon*), 306–10

Day, R.C., "Another Margot Chapter" (from *Quarterly West*), 332–45

Hoover, Judith, "Proteus" (from *Georgia Review*), 368–77

Phillips, Jayne Anne, "Lechery" (from *Persea: An International Review*), 381–88

Puig, Manuel, "From Kiss of the Spider Woman," trans. Thomas Colchie (from *Fiction*), 400–34

Reilly, Gary, "The Biography Man" (from *Iowa Review*), 441–50

Metcalf, Paul, "The Hat in the Swamp" (from *Milk Quarterly*), 472

Schutt, Christine, "These Women" (from *Gallimaufry*), 473–85

Neville, Susan Schaefer, "Johnny Appleseed" (from *Apalachee Quarterly*), 486–92

Gilchrist, Ellen, "Rich" (from *Intro*), 502–21

The Pushcart Prize, V: Best of the Small Presses (1980–81 Edition). Edited by Bill Henderson with the Pushcart Prize Editors, introduction by Bill Henderson (with comprehensive index to the series). Wainscott, NY: The Pushcart Press, 1980, cloth; New York: Avon, 1980, pb, 608 pp.

Short fiction contents:

Ozick, Cynthia, "Levitation" (from *Partisan Review*), 29–42

Shyne, Gerard, "Column Beda" (from *Under the Influence of Mal*, Inwood Press), 89–106

Ball, Bo, "Wish Book" (from *Chicago Review*), 124–35

Vaughn, Stephanie, "Sweet Talk" (from *Antaeus*), 201–11

Baber, Asa, "Tranquility Base" (from *fiction international*), 227–43

Wilbur, Ellen, "Faith" (from *Virginia Quarterly Review*), 275–86

Spencer, Elizabeth, "The Girl Who Loved Horses" (from *Ontario Review*), 320–37

Grossman, Barbara, "My Vegetable Love" (from *Paris Review*), 347–55

Bulatovic-Vib, Vlada, "The Shark and the Bureaucrat," trans. Nada Curcija-Prodanovic, (from *Modern Yugoslav Satire*), 356–57

Beriault, Gina, "The Infinite Passion of Expectation" (from *Ploughshares*), 360–67

Linney, Romulus, "How St. Peter Got Bald" (from *St. Andrew's Review*), 368–73

Feldman, Irving, "The Tortoise" (from *Canto*), 376

Madden, David, "On the Big Wind" (from *New Letters*), 377–96

Zelver, Patricia, "Story" (from *Ohio Review*), 399–402

Kinsella, W. P., "Pretend Dinners" (from *Crazyhorse*), 424–31

Vogan, Sara, "Scenes from the Homefront" (from *Antaeus*), 437–55

Brondoli, Michael, "Showdown" (from *Shenandoah*), 458–98

Francis, H. E., "Two Lives" (from *Kansas Quarterly*), 524–44

The Pushcart Prize, VI: Best of the Small Presses (1981–82 Edition). Edited by Bill Henderson, introduction by Bill Henderson (with index to the series). Wainscott, NY: The Pushcart Press, 1981, cloth; New York: Avon, 1981, pb, 540 pp.

Short fiction contents:

Whittier, Gayle, "Lost Time Accident" (from *Massachusetts Review*), 29–49

Ohle, David, "The Flocculus" (from *Paris Review*), 79–87

Carver, Raymond, "What We Talk About When We Talk About Love" (from *Antaeus*), 88–100

Thacker, Julia, "In Glory Land" (from *Antaeus*), 126–41

Silko, Leslie Marmon, "Coyote Holds a Full House in His Hand" (from *Triquarterly*), 142–50

Hejinian, Lyn, "Selections from *My Life*" (Burning Deck Press), 151–53

Targan, Barry, "Dominion" (from *Iowa Review*), 154–76

Engberg, Susan, "In the Land of Plenty" (from *Iowa Review*), 219–41

Goyen, William, "Arthur Bond" (from *Missouri Review*), 242–46

Tallent, Elizabeth Ann, "Why I Love Country Music" (from *Threepenny Review*), 247–57

Kiely, Benedict, "Fionn in the Valley" (from *Ploughshares*), 276–89
Antin(ova), Eleanor(a), "A Romantic Interlude" (from *Sun and Moon*), 289–303
Cassens, Denise, "Girl Talk" (from *Shankpainter*), 325–28
Phelan, Francis, "Four Ways of Computing Midnight" (from *Southern Review*), 338–85
Acker, Kathy, "New York City in 1979" (from *Crawl Out Your Window*), 396–412
Long, David, "Eclipse" (from *fiction international*), 413–28
Stafford, Jean, "Woden's Day" (from *Shenandoah*), 447–68
Shixu, Chen, "The General and the Small Town," trans. various translators (from *October*, China), 473–86

The Pushcart Prize, VII: Best of the Small Presses (1982–83 Edition). Edited by Bill Henderson with the Pushcart Prize Editors, introduction by Bill Henderson. Wainscott, NY: The Pushcart Press, 1982, cloth; New York: Avon, 1982, pb, 568 pp.

Short fiction contents:

Thompson, Barbara, "Tattoo" (from *Shenandoah*), 31–45
Davenport, Guy, "Christ Preaching at the Henley Regatta" (from *Eclogues*), 94–102
Ozick, Cynthia, "Helping T. S. Eliot Write Better" (from *American Poetry Review*), 103–12
Bedway, Barbara, "Death and Lebanon" (from *Iowa Review*), 118–28
Inness–Brown, Elizabeth, "Release, Surrender" (from *fiction international*), 150–58
Baxter, Charles, "Harmony of the World" (from *Michigan Quarterly Review*), 181–204
Selzer, Richard, "Mercy and the Witness" (from *Iowa Review*), 205–12
Oates, Joyce Carol, "Detente" (from *Southern Review*), 270–94
Licht, Fred, "Shelter the Pilgrim" (from *Hudson Review*), 324–41
Gilsen, William, "Getting Through It Together" (from Wickwire Press), 342–50
Phillips, Jayne Anne, "How Mickey Made It" (from Bookslinger Editions), 376–88
White, Edmund, "A Man of the World" (from *Shenandoah*), 394–413

Oz, Amos, "The Author Encounters his Reading Public," trans.
Nicholas deLange (from *Partisan Review*), 414–22

Robison, Mary, "Happy Boy, Allen" (from *Mississippi Review*),
449–58

Burgin, Richard, "Notes on Mrs. Slaughter" (from *Mississippi Review*), 464–76

The Pushcart Prize, VIII: Best of the Small Presses (1983–84 Edition). Edited by Bill Henderson with the Pushcart Prize Editors, introduction by Gail Godwin (with index to the series). Wainscott, NY: The Pushcart Press, 1983, cloth; New York: Avon, 1983, pb, 528 pp.

Short fiction contents:

Carver, Raymond, "A Small Good Thing" (from *Ploughshares*),
33–55

Johnson, Willis, "Prayer for the Dying" (from *Triquarterly*),
100–116

Lish, Gordon, "How to Write a Poem" (from *The Paris Review*),
145–49

Mason, Bobbie Ann, "Graveyard Day" (from *Ascent*), 156–67

McBrearty, Robert, "The Dishwasher" (from *Mississippi Review*),
168–73

Gilchrist, Ellen, "Summer, An Elegy" (from *Iowa Review*), 180–93

Codrescu, Andrei, "Samba de Los Agentes" (from *Paris Review*),
214–37

Wheeler, Kate, "Judgment" (from *Antaeus*), 275–88

Davidson, Jean, "Robo-Wash" (from *Mississippi Review*), 300–308

Becker, Jillian, "The Stench" (from *South African Jewish Voices*,
Micah Publishers), 309–38

Welch, Susan, "The Time, The Place, The Loved One" (from *Paris Review*), 347–67

Gass, William, "Some Snapshots from the Soviet Union" (from
Conjunctions), 384–97

Desaulniers, Janet, "Age" (from *Ploughshares*), 404–14

The Pushcart Prize, IX: Best of the Small Presses (1984–85 Edition). Edited by Bill Henderson with the Pushcart Prize Editors, introduction by Jayne Anne Phillips (with index to the series). Wainscott, NY: The Pushcart Press, 1984, cloth; New York: Avon, 1984, pb, 588 pp.

Short fiction contents:

Minot, Susan, "Hiding" (from *Grand Street*), 31–42

Porter, Joe Ashby, "Duckwalking" (from Sun and Moon Press), 70–75

Knowicki, Tadeusz, "From a Minor Apocalypse" (from *Triquarterly*), 83–102

Boyle, T. Coraghessan, "Caviar" (from *Anteaus*), 102–17

Yates, Richard, "Oh, Joseph, I'm So Tired" (from Wampeter Press), 132–54

Milton, Barbara, "The Cigarette Boat" (from Word Beat Press and *Paris Review*), 155–69

Thompson, Barbara, "Crossing" (from *Shenandoah*), 216–45

Sorrentino, Gilbert, "The Gala Cocktail Party" (from North Point Press and Sun and Moon Press), 246–51

Godwin, Gail, "Over the Mountain" (from *Antaeus*), 252–69

Malaparte, Curzio, "The Soroca Girls" (from Micah Publications), 276–88

Brown, Clark, "A Winter's Tale" (from *Writer's Forum*), 289–305

Carver, Raymond, "Careful" (from *Paris Review*), 306–16

Penner, Jonathan, "Emotion Recollected in Tranquility" (from *Quarterly West*), 335–43

Brandt, Pamela, "L.A. Child" (from *Story Quarterly*), 351–54

Keeley, Edmund, "Cambodian Diary" (from *Anteaus*), 355–404

Ruch, Teri, "Claire's Lover's Church" (from *Grand Street*), 462–69

Morris, Mary, "Copies" (from *Agni Review*), 506–17

Shannon, Beth Tashery, "Asilomarian Lecture (The Diurnal Life of the Inhabitants)" (from *Chicago Review*), 518–19

The Pushcart Prize, X: Best of the Small Presses (1985–86 Edition). Edited by Bill Henderson with the Pushcart Prize Editors, introduction by George Plimpton. Wainscott, NY: The Pushcart Press, 1985, cloth; New York: Avon, 1985, pb, 499 pp.

Short fiction contents:

O'Brien, Tim, "Quantum Jumps" (from *Ploughshares*), 3–31

Dybek, Stuart, "Hot Ice" (from *Antaeus*), 53–80

The Pushcart Prize, XI: Best of the Small Presses (1986–87 Edition). Edited by Bill Henderson with the Pushcart Prize Editors, introduction by Cynthia Ozick. Wainscott, NY: The Pushcart Press, 1986, cloth; New York: Avon, 1986, pb, 559 pp.

Short fiction contents:

The Pushcart Prize, XII: Best of the Small Presses (1987–88). Edited by Bill Henderson with the Pushcart Prize Editors, introduction by Frank Conroy. Wainscott, NY: The Pushcart Press, cloth; New York: Avon, 1987, pb, 559 pp.

Short fiction contents:

Adisa, Opal Palmer, "Duppy Get Her" (from *Bake-Face and Other Guava Stories*, Kelsey St. Press), 277–88

Brown, Rosellen, "One of Two" (from *New Letters*), 316–31

Ng, Rae Myenne, "A Red Sweater" (from *The American Voice*), 332–41

Jolley, Elizabeth, "My Father's Moon" (from *Grand Street*), 389–406

Emshwiller, Carol, "Yukon" (from *Triquarterly*), 407–14

West, Paul, "The Place in Flowers Where Pollen Rests" (*Conjunctions*), 430–42

Jaffe, Harold, "Persian Lamb" (from *Beasts*, Curbstone Press), 472–79

Gallagher, Tess, "The Lover of Horses" (from *Zyzzyva*), 480–91

The Pushcart Prize, XIII: Best of the Small Presses (1988–89 Edition). Edited by Bill Henderson with the Pushcart Prize Editors, introduction by Richard Ford. Wainscott, NY: The Pushcart Press, cloth; New York: Avon, 1988, pb, 475 pp.

Short fiction contents:

Bass, Rick, "Where the Sea Used to Be" (from *Paris Review*), 3–30

Gallagher, Tess, "Girls" (from *Milkweed Chronicle*), 50–64

Sandor, Marjorie, "Icarus Descending" (from *Antaeus*), 77–89

Spain, Chris, "Entrepreneurs" (from *The Quarterly*), 90–97

Birtha, Becky, "Johnnieruth" (from *Lover's Choice*, Seal Press), 138–43

Richard, Mark, "Happiness of the Garden Variety" (from *Shenandoah*), 144–56

Havazelet, Ehud, "What Is It Then Between Us?" (from *Ontario Review*), 179–86

Goldbarth, Albert, "After Yetzl" (from *Georgia Review*), 187–200

Godshalk, C.S., "Wonderland" (from *Iowa Review*), 215–29

Mairowitz, David Zane, "Hector Composes a Circular Letter" (from *Missouri Review*), 230–46

McFall, Lynne, "Star, Tree, Hand" (from *New England Review/Bread Loaf Quarterly*), 269–91

Rooke, Leon, "The Blue Baby" (from *Triquarterly*), 292–301

Abbott, Lee K., "The Era of Great Numbers" (from *Epoch*), 308–24

Shelnutt, Eve, "Andantino" (from *Western Humanities Review*), 325–35

Lentricchia, Melissa, "The Golden Robe" (from *fiction international*), 353–58

Castle, Sandi, "What the Shadow Knows" (from *Exquisite Corpse*), 388–92

Einzig, Barbara, "Life Moves Outside" (from *Life Moves Outside*, Burning Deck Press), 393–402

The Pushcart Prize, XIV: Best of the Small Presses (1989–90). Edited by Bill Henderson with the Pushcart Prize Editors, introduction by Tess Gallagher. Wainscott, NY: The Pushcart Press, cloth; New York: Avon, 1989, pb, 534 pp.

Short fiction contents:

MacLeod, Alistair, "Island" (from *Ontario Review*), 31–60

Martone, Michael, "The Safety Patrol" (from *Crescent Review*), 86–101

Wilson, Barbara, "Miss Venezuela" (from Seal Press), 124–39

Tysver, Peter, "After the Stations of the Cross" (from *The Quarterly*), 156–83

Nunez, Sigrid, "The Summer of the Hats" (from *Threepenny Review*), 196–209

Baxter, Charles, "Westland" (from *Paris Review*), 212–30

Davis, Lydia, "Five Stories" (from *Conjunctions*), 233–46

McGrath, Kristina, "Housework" (from *The American Voice*), 267–78

Schwartz, Sheila, "Mutatis Mutandis" (from *Crazyhorse*), 280–305

Minkoff, Robert, "Better Tomorrow" (from *New England Review/Bread Loaf Quarterly*), 324–32

Bowles, Paul, "Tangier, 1975" (from *Unwelcome Words*, Tombouctou Books), 335–40

Tanner, Ron, "Garbage" (from *Iowa Review*), 343–9

Henry, DeWitt, "Witness" (from *Boulevard*), 355–78

Oates, Joyce Carol, "Party" (from *Boston Review*), 381–84

Huss, Sandy, "Coupon for Blood" (from *Triquarterly*), 387–400

Goodison, Lorna, "By Love Possessed" (from *Callaloo*), 419–24

Jauss, David, "Freeze" (from *New England Review/Bread Loaf Quarterly*), 433–47

Manley, Frank, "The Rain of Terror" (from *The Southern Review*), 453–74

The Pushcart Prize, XV: Best of the Small Presses (1990–91 Edition). Edited by Bill Henderson with the Pushcart Prize Editors, introduction by Russell Banks: Wainscott, NY: The Pushcart Press, cloth; New York: Avon, 1990, pb, 581 pp.

Short fiction contents:

Bass, Rick, "Wejumpka" (from *Chariton Review*), 451–59
Bly, Carol, "My Lord Bag of Rice" (from *Laurel Review*), 464–85
Kalpakian, Laura, "The Battle of Manila" (from *Iowa Review*), 490–515

AUTHOR INDEX

McBrearty, Robert. "The Dishwasher." VIII:1983–84, 168–73.
McFall, Lynne. "Star, Tree, Hand." XIII:1988–89, 269–91.
McGrath, Kristina, "Housework." XIV:1989–90, 267–78.
Metcalf, Paul. "The Hat in the Swamp." IV:1979–80, 472.
Milton, Barbara. "The Cigarette Boat." IX:1984–85, 155–69.
Minkoff, Robert. "Better Tomorrow." XIV:1989–90, 324–32.
Minot, Susan. "Hiding." IX:1984–85, 31–42.
Morris, Mary. "Copies." IX:1984–85, 506–17.
Muravin, Victor. "The Red Cross Night." II:1977–78, 78–90.

Nations, Opal. "The U.S. Chinese Immigrant's Book of the Art of
    Sex." II:1977–78, 310–16.
Nelson, Kent. "The Middle of Nowhere." XV:1990–91, 306–23.
Neville, Susan Schaefer. "Johnny Appleseed." IV:1979–80, 486–92.
Ng, Fae Myenne. "A Red Sweater." XII:1987–88, 332–41.
Nin, Anaïs. "Waste of Timelessness." III:1978–79, 312–16.
Novakovich, Josip. "Rust." XV:1990–91, 69–81.
Nunez, Sigrid. "The Summer of the Hats." XIV:1989–90, 196–209.

Oates, Joyce Carol. "Détente." VII:1982–83, 270–94.
———. "The Hallucination." I:1976–77, 404–16.
———. "Party." XIV:1989–90, 381–84.
O'Brien, Tim. "Going after Caccioto." 1977–78, 53–71.
———. "Quantum Jumps." X:1985–86, 3–31.
Ohle, David. "The Boy Scout." II:1977–78, 465–67.
———. "The Flocculus." VI:1981–82, 79–87.
Oz, Amos. "The Author Encounters His Reading Public." (trans.
    Nicholas de Lange). VII:1982–83, 414–22.
Ozick, Cynthia. "Helping T. S. Eliot Write Better." VII:1982–83,
    103–12.
———. "Levitation." V:1980–81, 29–41.

Payerle, George. "Wolfbane Fane." III:1978–79, 318–21.
Penner, Jonathan. "Emotion Recollected in Tranquility."
    IX:1984–85, 335–43.
Petersen, Mary. "To Dance." III:1978–79, 143–51.
Phelan, Francis. "Four Ways of Computing Midnight." VI:1981–82,
    338–85.
Phillips, Jayne Anne. "Home." IV:1979–80, 29–42.
———. "How Mickey Made It." VII:1982–83, 376–88.
———. "Lechery." IV:1979–80, 381–88.
———. "Sweethearts." II:1977–78, 317–20.
Pilcrow, John. "Turtle." III:1978–79, 458.

Porter, Joe Ashby. "Duckwalking." IX:1984–85, 70–75.
———. "Sweetness, A Thinking Machine." IV:1979–80, 306–10.
Poverman, C. E. "Beautiful." XII:1987–88, 259–76.
Powell, Padgett. "Typical." XV:1990–91, 58–68.
Prose, Francine. "Other Lives." XI:1986–87, 45–58.
Puig, Manual. "From Kiss of the Spider Woman." IV:1979–80,
    400–34.
Pulaski, Jack. "Father of the Bride." I:1976–77, 218–26.

Ratushinskaia, Irina. "On the Meaning of Life." (trans. Diane
    Nemec Ignashev). XII:1987–88, 46–49.
Reilly, Gary. "The Biography Man." IV:1979–80, 441–50.
Reyzen, Avrom. "The Dog." I:1976–77, 115–21.
Richard, Mark. "Happiness of the Garden Variety." XIII:1988–89,
    144–56.
Rios, Alberto Alvaro. "The Secret Lion." X:1985–86, 159–64.
Robison, Mary. "Happy Boy, Allen." VII:1982–83, 449–58.
Rooke, Leon. "The Blue Baby." XIII:1988–89, 292–301.
Ruch, Teri. "Claire's Lover's Church." IX:1984–85, 462–69.

Sanders, Ed. "The Mother-in-Law." I:1976–77, 248–54.
Sandor, Marjorie. "Icarus Descending." XIII:1988–89, 77–89.
Sanford, John. "The Fire at the Catholic Church." II:1977–78, 3–84.
Savory, Teo. "The Monk's Chimera." II:1977–78, 396–99.
Schott, Max. "Early Winter." IV:1979–80, 239–66.
Schutzman, Steve. "The Bank Robbery." II:1977–78, 467–69.
Schutt, Christine. "These Women." IV:1979–80, 473–85.
Schwartz, Lynne Sharon. "Rough Strife." III:1978–79, 29–48.
Schwartz, Sheila. "Mutatis Mutandis." XIV:1989–90, 280–305.
Selzer, Richard. "Mercy and the Witness." VII:1982–83, 205–12.
Shacochis, Bob. "Hot Day on the Gold Coast." X:1985–86, 333–56.
Shannon, Beth Tashery. "Asilomarian Lecture (The Dermal Life of
    the Inhabitants)." IX:1984–85, 518–19.
———. "Bons." III:1978–79, 73–75.
Shelnutt, Eve. "Andantino." XIII:1988–89, 325–35.
Shixu, Chen. "The General and the Small Town." (trans. various
    translators). VI:1981–82, 473–86.
Shyne, Gerard. "Column Beda." V:1980–81, 89–106.
Silko, Leslie Marmon. "Coyote Holds a Full House in his Hand."
    VI:1981–82, 142–50.
Simpson, Mona. "Lawns." XI:1986–87, 3–22.

TITLE INDEX (BY STORY)

American Fiction Series, 1987–90

Another individual initiative like the *Pushcart Prize*, and the most recent of the series included in this book, the *American Fiction* series was started in 1987 by Michael C. White, a professor at Springfield College in Massachusetts. His aim was to combine the best of the well-known fiction anthologies (*Best American Short Stories, O. Henry Award, Editor's Choice*) with a more open, more direct call for unpublished manuscripts to the writers themselves.

Unlike *Best American Short Stories* and *O. Henry, American Fiction* is not a reprint series but an annual volume of previously unpublished short stories collected nationally from both known and unknown authors and selected through a competitive double screening process. The solicitation takes the form of advertisements inviting submissions (and the payment of a $7.50 entry fee). The many hundreds of entries received are narrowed by White and co-editor Alan Davis to a short list, from which a well-known judge selects the three "winning" stories. The three winners receive a cash prize and are published, along with all the short-listed finalists, in the volume. The finalists are also paid a modest honorarium.

For the first three years, the series was published by White himself (as distinct from vanity publishing), but in 1989 the series was picked up by Birch Lane Press (a subsidiary of Carroll

Communications in New York City), which has published the volumes since, giving the authors prominent national exposure in a well-produced, well-distributed book.

While such publication auspices may seem prestigious, the *American Fiction Series* also holds a certain disadvantage from the writer's point of view. He or she is required to relinquish copyright to the story, assigning it to White and Davis, an unusual feature that leaves the future of the series open to question. Nonetheless, the first four volumes have showcased nearly eighty distinguished stories, and in the future this unusual practice of copyright assignment will probably give way to a more writer-friendly frame for this otherwise fine series.

Ann Beattie, Raymond Carver, Anne Tyler, and Louise Erdrich have been guest judges for the first four volumes. Among the mostly unknown writers published in the series are a few more prominent names, such as the director of the Milkweed National Fiction Competition, Emily Meier, and the former head of the National Endowment for the Arts, Joe David Bellamy (neither of whom, I should add, made it into the winner's circle). Also included are writers who went on to win further awards and prominence, such as Antonya Nelson, Cris Mazza, and Perry Glasser.

CHRONOLOGICAL INDEX WITH STORY CONTENTS

American Fiction 87. Edited by Michael C. White and Alan Davis, introduction by Ann Beattie. Hartford, CT: Wesley Press, 1987, pb, 197 pp.

Contents:

Cooper, Stephen, "Threshold," 131–42
Henley, Patricia, "The Late Hunt," 143–52
Feingold, Carol Magun, "Avner," 153–62
Tracy, Stephen, "In a Family Way," 163–78
Bradway, Becky, "The Princess Bed," 179–94

American Fiction 88. Edited by Michael C. White and Alan Davis, introduction by Raymond Carver. Farmington, CT: Wesley Press, 1988, pb, 228 pp.

Contents:

Nelson, Antonya, "The Expendables" (First Prize), 1–16
Malone, Paul Scott, "Bringing Joby Back" (Second Prize), 17–32
Dorr, Sandra, "Writing in the Dark" (Third Prize), 33–44
Hegi, Ursula, "Saving a Life," 45–54
Page, Patricia, "Escapade," 55–64
Robertson, Mary Elsie, "Parting Words," 65–80
Blaine, Michael, "Suits," 81–90
Vinz, Mark, "Almost October," 91–98
Trussell, Donna, "Dream Pie," 99–110
Driscoll, Scott, "Waiting for the Bus," 111–22
Harrison, Pat, "The Winner," 123–32
Jackson, Gordon, "In the Garden," 133–42
Graham, Toni, "Jump!", 143–54
Hettick, Michael, "Angels," 155–64
Tana, Patti, "Harbor Island," 165–68
Tanner, Ron, "The Hart House," 169–78
Tracy, Stephen, "Fools' Experiments," 179–94
Zeiger, Lila, "Fine Details," 195–206
Becker, Leslee, "The Funny Part," 207–24

American Fiction Number 1, The Best Unpublished Stories by Emerging Writers. Edited by Michael C. White and Alan Davis, introduction by Anne Tyler. New York: Birch Lane Press/Carol Publishing Group, 1990, pb, 395 pp.

Contents:

McMillan, Florri, "The Color of Scars" (First Prize), 7–23
Browder, Catherine, "Tigers" (Second Prize), 24–42
Mason, David, "Pullandbedamned Point" (Third Prize), 43–59

Hershman, Marcie, "Sworn Statement: The Map," 60–77
Ruiter, Jane, "Trees," 78–84
Evans, Elizabeth, "Ransom," 85–98
Kennedy, Thomas E., "Little Sinners," 99–112
Hegi, Ursula, "Baby Mansion," 113–25
Kobin, Joann, "His Mother, His Daughter," 126–36
Gill, Jelena Bulat, "Nobody under the Rose," 137–56
Harrison, Pat, "Elevator Man," 157–69
Higgins, Joanna, "Dancing at the Holland," 170–84
Mazza, Cris, "Is It Sexual Harassment Yet?", 185–204
Nieker, Mark, "Elvis," 205–20
Morse, David, "The Eelskin Jumpsuit," 221–37
Goldberg, Maria Noell, "By Indian Time," 238–49
Lewis, Robin, "Jet Pilot for the Sandinistas," 250–67
Unger, Barbara, "The Gambler's Daughter," 268–82
Bellamy, Joe David, "1963," 283–98
Bradway, Becky, "Looking for the New Year," 299–311
Bennet, Sally, "The Crossing," 312–33
Copeland, Ann, "Leaving the World," 334–51
Huckle, Susan S., "Plans," 352–69
Morrow, Diane Stelzer, "Lourdes," 370–91

American Fiction 2, The Best Unpublished Stories by Emerging Writers. Edited by Michael C. White and Alan Davis, introduction by Louise Erdrich. New York: Birch Lane Press/Carol Publishing Group, 1991, pb, 306 pp.

Contents:

McCown, Clint, "Home Course Advantage" (First Prize), 1–16
Donovan, Heather Baird, "Basin and Range" (Second Prize), 17–35
Cole, David, "Being There Is Good for the Children" (Third Prize), 36–49
Diogenes, Marvin, "*Forbrengen*" (Honorable Mention), 50–71
Sheffer, Roger, "Korean Lessons," 72–87
Glasser, Perry, "Recapitulation," 88–101
Peterson, Karen, "Wild Hearts," 102–20
Kobin, Joann, "Wildlife," 121–134
Troy, Mary, "Henrietta," 135–47
Camillo, Barbara Asch, "Weigh Station," 148–59

AUTHOR INDEX

TITLE INDEX (BY STORY)

"Korean Lessons," Roger Sheffer. AF2, 72–87.

"Late Hunt, The," Patricia Henley. AF87, 143–52.
"Leaving the World," Ann Copeland. AF1, 334–51.
"Little Sinners," Thomas E. Kennedy. AF1, 99–112.
"Looking for Frank," Diane Sherry Case. AF2, 288–306.
"Looking for the New Year," Becky Bradway. AF1, 299–311.
"Lost Chords," Burton Raffel. AF87, 87–96.
"Lourdes," Diane Stelzer Morrow. AF1, 370–91.

"Mexico," Jeanne McDonald. AF87, 13–26.
"Ms. Skywriter, Inc.," William Babula. AF87, 121–30.
"Museum of Ordinary People, The," Lewis Turco. AF2, 220–28.
"My Father Mad and Laughing," Nicholas Rinaldi. AF87, 57–68.

"Naked Woman," Joy Tremewan. AF2, 209–19.
"1963," Joe David Bellamy. AF1, 283–98.
"Nobody under the Rose," Jelena Bulat Gill. AF1, 137–56.

"Parting Words," Mary Elsie Robertson. AF88, 65–80.
"Pictures of Silver, Pictures of Gold," Jonathan Maney. AF2,
      160–73.
"Plans," Susan S. Huckle. AF1, 352–69.
"Princess Bed, The," Becky Bradway. AF87, 179–94.
"Pullandbedamned Point," David Mason. AF1, 43–59.

"Ransom," Elizabeth Evans. AF1, 85–98.
"Recapitulation," Perry Glasser. AF2, 88–101.
"Rituals," Marilyn K. Krueger. AF2, 174–9.

"Salvaging," Ingrid Smith. AF87, 69–86.
"Saving a Life," Ursula Hegi. AF88, 45–54.
"Sea Turtles," Jeanne McDonald. AF87, 97–110.
"Suits," Michael Blaine. AF88, 81–90.
"Sworn Statement: The Map," Marcie Hershman. AF1, 60–77.

"Tape Recorder, The," Timothy Kelley. AF87, 1–12.
"Threshold," Stephen Cooper. AF87, 131–42.
"Tigers," Catherine Browder. AF1, 24–42.
"Trees," Jane Ruiter. AF1, 78–84.

"Waiting for the Bus," Scott Driscoll. AF88, 111–22.

II. Series of Single-Author Collections

Associated Writing Programs Short Fiction Award, 1978–90

Drue Heinz Literature Prize, 1981–90

Flannery O'Connor Award, 1983–90

University of Illinois Series, 1975–90

Iowa School of Letters Award, 1970–90

Associated Writing Programs Short Fiction Award, 1978–90

The Associated Writing Programs (AWP), housed at Old Dominion University, Norfolk, Virginia, is an affiliation of several hundred college and university writing programs in the United States.

Each year since 1978, AWP has sponsored a literary competition for book-length works in three categories: the novel, poetry, and short fiction. The short fiction collection entries are screened from among the manuscripts submitted to the competition by a panel of fiction writers. The author of the winning volume receives a cash award, and the collection is published by the University of Missouri Press. In addition to choosing winners, the judges are free to select finalists; AWP serves as a literary agent, seeking to place finalist manuscripts with a publisher. In 1979, for example, the finalist entry by Gladys Swan, *On the Edge of the Desert*, was recommended by judge Gordon Weaver to the University of Illinois Press, which ultimately published the work in its short fiction series (also featured in this volume). While that was her first book publication, Swan went on to distinguish herself with several further collections and novels. More than fifty books have been published as a result of the AWP's efforts.

The distinguished judges for the series have included Wallace Stegner, Richard Yates, Joyce Carol Oates, Raymond Carver, Donald Barthelme, Paul Bowles, Ann Beattie (who chose *not* to give an award), Robley Wilson, Jr., François Camoin, David Huddle, and Charles Baxter. The names of several of the winners have also grown prominent in the literary world—including Camoin and Baxter.

Winners of the AWP Short Fiction Award, all books published by University of Missouri Press, Columbia, MO 65205.

CHRONOLOGICAL INDEX WITH STORY CONTENTS

1978: *The Further Adventures of Brunhild*, Rebecca Kavaler. Judge: Wallace Stegner.

Contents:

"Director's Notes," 1
"The Further Adventures of Brunhild," 19
"The Chambered Nautilus," 42
"Give Brother My Best," 73
"Ariadne," 92
"Compensation Claim," 112
"Stillbirth," 122
"The Meat Eaters," 136

1979: *Light and Power*, Ian MacMillan (published 1980). Judge: Richard Yates.

Contents:

"The Rock," 1
"The Rat's Eye," 14
"Light and Power," 25
"Ashes," 41
"Idiot's Rebellion," 47
"The Gravity of the Situation," 63
"Corrigan's Progress," 78
"Sacrifice," 88
"The Drive," 96

1980: ***Metaphysical Tales***, Eugene Garber. Judge: Joyce Carol Oates.

Contents:

Foreword by Joyce Carol Oates, vii
"The Poets," 1
"The Lover," 26
"The Host," 44
"Malagueña," 68
"The Women," 100
"Metaphysical Tales:"
   "The Melon-eaters," 117
   "Selections from The Assassin's Memoirs," 133
   "White Monkey Man," 140
"The Black Prince," 152
"The Prisoner," 165
"The Child," 173
"The Gamblers," 181

1981: ***The End of the World Is Los Angeles***, François Camoin (published 1982). Judge: Stanley Elkin.

Contents:

"Lieberman's Father," 1
"Things I Did to Make It Possible," 15
"Teller, the Bear and the Yellow Thunderbird," 19
"Drowning in California," 28
"Superman (Georgia's Dream)," 40
"The Vanishing," 47
"A Grown Man," 56
"A Marriage," 62
"Now She Sleeps," 71
"My Life Is a Screenplay," 85

1982: ***Delta q***, Alvin Greenburg (published 1983). Judge: Raymond Carver.

Contents:

I. Momentum
"The Power of Language," 3

"Game Time," 23
"The Serious World and Its Environs," 38
"The Main Chance," 51
"Dear Ones," 68
"The Ascent of Man," 87
"The State of the Art," 95
II. Position
"Delta q," 111
"Leanings," 121
"Myopia," 127
"To Be or Not To Be," 147
"Disorder and Belated Sorrow: A Shadow Play," 157
"Who Is This Man and What Is He Doing in My Life?", 166
"Not a Story by Isaac Bashevis Singer," 181

1983: ***Harmony of the World***, Charles Baxter (published 1984). Judge: Donald Barthelme.

Contents:

"Gershwin's Second Prelude," 1
"Xavier Speaking," 17
"The Model," 36
"Horace and Margaret's Fifty-second," 44
"The Cliff," 59
"A Short Course in Nietzschean Ethics," 63
"The Would-be Father," 79
"Weights," 95
"Harmony of the World," 111
"The Crank," 136

1984: ***Off in Zimbabwe***, Rod Kessler (published 1985). Judge: Paul Bowles.

Contents:

"Lieutenant," 1
"A Bad Winter Just East of Show Low," 12
"An Infidelity," 21
"Mailman," 32
"Benny and I," 37
"How to Touch a Bleeding Dog," 46

"Dos Serpientes," 48
"A Member of the Class," 64
"The Death of Rodney Snee," 67
"Another Thursday with the Meyerhoffs," 73
"Off in Zimbabwe," 78
"Carter," 88
"Victoria and Jerry," 91
"My Name Is Buddy," 102
"October Reeds," 107

1985: No award. Judge: Ann Beattie.

1986: ***The Dogeater: Stories***, Jesse Lee Kercheval (published 1987). Judge: Robley Wilson, Jr., and Irene Skolnick.

Contents:

"Underground Women," 1
"Willy," 10
"A Clean House," 20
"Tertiary Care," 32
"La Mort au Moyen Âge," 41
"The History of the Church in America," 48
"A History of Indiana," 67
"The Dogeater," 78

1987: ***Basic Skills***, Anne Finger (published 1988). Judge: François Camoin.

Contents:

"Cross-Country," 1
"Like the Hully-Gully but Not So Slow," 18
"Abortion," 37
"A Tragedy," 55
"Basic Skills," 75
"Cars," 91
"Old Maids," 99

1988: ***Things We Lose***, Roland Sodowsky (published 1989). Judge: David Huddle.

Contents:

1989: ***Walking on Ice***, Susan Hubbard (published 1990). Judge: Charles Baxter.

Contents:

AUTHOR INDEX

Drue Heinz Literature Prize, 1981–90

I happened to be with Walter Wetherell in Vermont in early January 1985 when he received notice that his collection, *The Man Who Loved Levittown*, had been selected by Max Appel for the Drue Heinz Prize. The first words I heard from him were, "Well, that proves it's not fixed."

Although I had never heard of the prize before, I have since come to see it as one of the most prestigious awards offered for the short story in the United States (the cash prize itself is one of the highest). Wetherell's exclamation underscores the sincerity of the screening judges. The prize is awarded not by a club of old boys—as is the case in some competitions—but by individuals who love the short story, recognizing what they deem the best of the works submitted and focusing on the stories themselves, without regard for the celebrity of the author.

The prize was established in 1980 by the Howard Heinz Endowment and the University of Pittsburgh Press to honor high-quality short fiction. Mrs. H. J. Heinz initiated the Prize to fill what she perceived as a gap in the spectrum of literary awards—to provide something for the new, not well-established short story writers who had begun to publish but were not yet well established. (Mrs. Heinz has also extended support to the literary journal *Antaeus* and the Ecco Press.)

The Heinz prize competition has been judged by a number of distinguished writers, including Robert Penn Warren, Raymond Carver, Wright Morris, Joyce Carol Oates, Max Appel, Alison Lurie, Nadine Gordimer, Margaret Atwood, and Robert Coover.

Winners of the Drue Heinz Literature Prize, all published by University of Pittsburgh Press, Pittsburgh, PA 15260.

CHRONOLOGICAL INDEX WITH STORY CONTENTS

1981: ***The Death of Descartes***, David Bosworth. Senior Judge: Robert Penn Warren.

Contents:

"Excerpts from a Report of the Commission," 1
"Psalm," 27
"Dice," 49
"Alien Life," 69
"The Death of Descartes," 105

1982: ***Dancing for Men***, Robley Wilson, Jr. Senior Judge: Raymond Carver.

Contents:

"Despair," 3
"Dancing for Men," 11
"Thief," 27
"Artists and Their Models," 31
"Pieces of String," 4
   "1. Crossings," 43
   "2. A Story with Sex and Violence," 44
   "3. Fashion," 45
   "4. Children," 46
   "5. Mothers," 48
   "6. The Hundred Steps," 48
"Wasps," 51
"A Fear of Children," 61
"Land Fishers," 79

"Thalia," 99
"An Inward Generation," 105
  "1. Meadow Green, 1939," 105
  "2. Business, 1947," 108
  "3. War Games, 1952," 125
  "4. The Cause, 1962," 130
  "5. Proposing, 1975," 136
"Paint," 143

1983: ***Private Parties***, Jonathan Penner. Senior Judge: Wright Morris.

Contents:

"Men Are of Three Kinds," 3
"Uncle Hersh," 11
"Things to be Thrown Away," 25
"A Way of Life," 33
"Frankenstein Meets the Ant People," 49
"Emotion Recollected in Tranquillity," 63
"At Center," 77
"Investments," 91
"Shrinkage," 105
"Temblor," 119
"Sailing Home," 143
"Articles on the Heart," 161
"Harry and Maury," 169
"Amarillo," 187

1984: ***The Luckiest Man in the World***, Randall Silvis. Senior Judge: Joyce Carol Oates.

Contents:

"The Luckiest Man in the World," 3
"Trash Man," 63
"Prayer and Old Jokes," 79
"One Night with a Girl by the Seine," 131
"A Walk in the Moonlight," 161
"The Fatalist," 183

1985: **The Man Who Loved Levittown**, W. D. Wetherell. Senior Judge: Max Apple.

Contents:

"The Man Who Loved Levittown," 3
"If a Woodchuck Could Chuck Wood," 23
"The Lob," 39
"The Bass, the River, and Sheila Mant," 57
"Nickel a Throw," 65
"Why I Love America," 79
"Narrative of the Whale Truck Essex," 95
"Volpi's Farewell," 103
"North of Peace," 113
"Spitfire Autumn," 125

1986: **Under the Wheat**, Rick DeMarinis. Senior Judge: Alison Lurie.

Contents:

"Under the Wheat," 1
"Good Wars," 21
"The Smile of a Turtle," 47
"Weeds," 59
"Life Between Meals," 81
"Blind Euchre," 103
"Billy Ducks Among the Pharaohs," 127

1987: **In the Music Library**, Ellen Hunnicutt. Senior Judge: Nadine Gordimer.

Contents:

"At St. Theresa's College for Women," 3
"There is a Balm in Gilead," 17
"All Kinds of Flowers," 27
"Energy," 43
"Bargaining," 53
"In the Music Library," 65
"A Hidden Thing," 75
"Bringing the News," 87
"Amos," 97

"When I Was Married," 125
"The Bengal Tiger," 133

1988: ***Moustapha's Eclipse***, Reginald McKnight. Senior Judge: Margaret Atwood.

Contents:

"Mali is Very Dangerous," 3
"First I Look at the Purse," 17
"Peaches," 27
"Who Big Bob?" 37
"Uncle Moustapha's Eclipse," 43
"Gettin' to Be Like the Studs," 53
"The Voice," 63
"The Honey Boys," 79
"How I Met Idi at the Bassi Dakaru Restaurant," 103
"Rebirth," 115

1989: ***Cartographies***, Maya Sonenberg. Senior Judge: Robert Coover.

Contents:

"Cartographies," 3
"Quarry Games," 23
"Nature Morte," 35
"Secession," 43
"Ashes," 63
"Ariadne in Exile," 71
"June 4, 1469," 95
"Interval," 115
"Afterimage," 127
"Dioramas," 137

1990: ***Limbo River***, Rick Hillis. Senior Judge: Russell Banks.

Contents:

"Blue," 3
"The Eve," 23

AUTHOR INDEX

TITLE INDEX (BY COLLECTION)

Man Who Loved Levittown, The, W. D. Wetherell. 1985.
Moustapha's Eclipse, Reginald McKnight. 1988.

Private Parties, Jonathan Penner. 1983.

Under the Wheat, Rick DeMarinis. 1986.

Flannery O'Connor Award, 1983–90

The Flannery O'Connor Award for Short Fiction was established by the University of Georgia Press in 1981, the two winners for that year being published in 1983. Paul Zimmer, then Director of the University of Georgia Press, conceived of the series and award. In 1984 Zimmer went on to head the University of Iowa Press, which publishes the *Iowa School of Letters Award* (also included in this volume).

Charles East, who had been in charge of the short fiction program at the Louisiana State University Press in the sixties and seventies—a program of open submissions, not a competition—took on responsibility for the Flannery O'Connor series from the start, both as judge and editor. When East retired from Georgia at the end of 1983, he was invited to continue to run the O'Connor series from his home in Baton Rouge.

From the award's inception up to 1987, East read all of the several hundred submissions (typically 300–400 per year), selected the ten finalists, and engaged an established short-story writer to serve as final judge. Since 1987, however, the selection process has been performed by three or four writers, who select a short list of fifteen or twenty finalists from whom East himself picks the two co-winners.

A glance at the names of the twenty-one winners to date (four were selected in 1984) shows mostly writers who were unknown before winning, although a number have gone on to achieve some prominence in the field. A few of the winners have been fairly well-known writers such as Daniel Curley and François Camoin, who also won the AWP series in 1981.

Winners of the Flannery O'Connor Award for Short Fiction, all published by the University of Georgia Press, Athens, GA 30602.

CHRONOLOGICAL INDEX WITH STORY CONTENTS

(N.B.: year shown is year of publication, not necessarily the year of award—in most cases, unless otherwise indicated, the actual year of award is one year earlier than the publication year.)

1983: *Evening Out*, David Walton

Contents:

"Evening Out," 11
"Moogle Boogled," 37
"Synaphongenuphon," 51
"The Gingerbread House," 69
"Skin and Bone," 99
"Easy to Believe," 145
"The Lid," 163
"The Sundeck," 181

1983: *From the Bottom Up*, Leigh Allison Wilson

Contents:

"From the Bottom Up," 1
"Mildred Motley and the Son of a Bitch," 12
"The Raising," 21
"The Snipe Hunters," 38
"Invictus," 52
"South of the Border," 63

1984: *Close-Ups*, Sandra Thompson

Contents:

1984: *The Invention of Flight*, Susan Neville

Contents:

1984: *How Far She Went*, Mary Hood

Contents:

"Lonesome Road Blues," 1
"Solomon's Seal," 22
"A Man Among Men," 30
"A Country Girl," 49
"How Far She Went," 67
"Doing This, Saying That, to Applause," 78
"Manly Conclusions," 83
"Hindsight," 93
"Inexorable Progress," 102

1984: *Why Men Are Afraid of Women*, François Camoin

Contents:

"Miami," 1
"It Could Happen," 14
"Peacock Blue," 40
"Diehl: The Wandering Years," 51
"A Special Case," 67
"Home Is the Blue Moon Cafe," 79
"The Amelia Barons," 92
"A Hunk of Burning Love," 105
"La Vida," 115
"Cheerful Wisdom," 129
"Sometimes the Wrong Thing Is the Right Thing," 138

1985: *Rough Translations*, Molly Giles

Contents:

"Old Souls," 1
"A Jar of Emeralds," 10
"Heart and Soul," 19
"How to Quit Smoking," 29
"Baby Pictures," 40
"Chocolate Footballs," 52
"The Planter Box," 70
"Pie Dance," 77
"What Do You Say?" 86
"Peril," 95

"Self-Defense," 107
"Rough Translations," 120

1985: *Living with Snakes*, Daniel Curley

Contents:

"Trinity," 1
"The Inlet," 13
"The Other Two," 26
"Revenge," 41
"Wild Geese," 50
"Reflections in the Ice," 58
"Living with Snakes," 71
"The First Baseman," 84
"The Contrivance," 93
"Billy Will's Song," 107
"Visiting the Dead," 120

1986: *The Piano Tuner*, Peter Meinke

Contents:

I Home Thoughts
"The Piano Tuner," 3
"Alice's Brother," 15
"Ruby Lemons," 23
"The Ponŏes," 34
"Conversation with a Pole," 46
"Losers Pay," 58
"Even Crazy Old Barmaids Need Love," 71
II From Abroad
"A Decent Life," 85
"The Twisted River," 97
"Sealink," 108
"The Starlings of Leicester Square," 117
"Winter Term," 122
"The Water-Tree," 134
"The Bracelet," 144

1986: *The Evening News*, Tony Ardizzone

Contents:

1987: *The Boys of Bensonhurst*, Salvatore La Puma

Contents:

1987: *Spirit Seizures*, Melissa Pritchard

Contents:

1988: *Silent Retreats*, Philip F. Deaver

Contents:

1988: *The Purchase of Order*, Gail Galloway Adams

Contents:

1989: *Useful Gifts*, Carole L. Glickfeld

Contents:

1990: *The Expendables*, Antonya Nelson

Contents:

1990: *The People I Know*, Nancy Zafris

Contents:

1990: *The Source of Trouble*, Debra Monroe

Contents:

1991: ***Ghost Traps***, Robert H. Abel (1989 award)

Contents:

1991: ***Low Flying Aircraft***, T. M. McNally (1990 award)

Contents:

1992: *The Melancholy of Departure*, Alfred DePew (1990 award)

Contents:

Hood, Mary. *How Far She Went*. 1984.

La Pume, Salvatore. *The Boys of Bensonhurst*. 1987.

McNally, T. M. *Low Flying Aircraft*. 1990.
Meinke, Peter. *The Piano Tuner*. 1986.
Monroe, Debra. *The Source of Trouble*. 1989.

Nelson, Antonya. *The Expendables*. 1990.
Neville, Susan. *The Invention of Flight*. 1984.

Pritchard, Melissa. *Spirit Seizures*. 1987.

Thompson, Sandra. *Close-Ups*. 1984.

Walton, David. *Evening out*. 1983.
Wilson, Leigh Allison. *From the Bottom Up*. 1983.

Zafris, Nancy. *The People I Know*. 1990.

TITLE INDEX (BY COLLECTION)

Melancholy of Departure, The, Alfred DePew. 1992.

People I Know, The, Nancy Zafris. 1990.
Piano Tuner, The, Peter Meinke. 1986.
Purchase of Order, The, Gail Galloway Adams. 1988.

Rough Translations, Molly Giles. 1985.

Silent Retreats, Philip F. Deaver. 1988.
Source of Trouble, The, Debra Monroe. 1990.
Spirit Seizures, Melissa Pritchard. 1987.

Useful Gifts, Carole Glickfeld. 1989.

Why Men Are Afraid of Women, François Camoin. 1984.

University Of Illinois Short Fiction
Series, 1975–90

At the beginning of the 1970s, the University of Illinois issued, as a trial run for an ongoing series, three story collections by local writers, two of whom, Dan Curley and Paul Friedman, went on ultimately to join the regular series, while the third, Mark Costello, became well known for his collection, *The Murphy Stories*, which continues to be Illinois' best-selling collection.

With the success of these three collections, it seemed only logical that an annual series should begin, and in 1975 the first four volumes of the University of Illinois Short Fiction Series were published simultaneously. The series was initiated by the director of the Press, Richard L. Wentworth, who had instituted a short fiction series at Louisiana State University in the 1960s when he directed LSU Press (see the section of this volume dealing with the Flannery O'Connor Short Fiction Award).

Between 1975 and 1990, fifty-seven collections appeared, making this by far the most prolific single-author short-fiction program of the five included in this volume. The Illinois program is not a competition, per se. Selections are made on the basis of recommendations (for example, Gordon Weaver recommended Gladys Swan, and

George Core, editor of *Sewanee Review*, recommended Susan Engberg, William Hoffman, Rebecca Kavaler, Kermit Moyer, Helen Norris, and Barry Targan), as well as by direct submission. Collections submitted are read by one of the Press's outside readers for recommendation—the names of the outside readers are not revealed.

In 1988 the Press issued an anthology of stories selected from the series, entitled *Prime Number: 17 Stories from Illinois Short Fiction*, which is listed with the other volumes in this series. The anthology was edited jointly by series editor Ann Lowry Weir and George Core. It gives a good sampling of the stories published over the years in the Series.

University of Illinois Short Fiction Series, all published by the University of Illinois Press, Urbana and Chicago, IL 61820.

CHRONOLOGICAL INDEX WITH STORY CONTENTS

1975

Crossings, Stephen Minot

Contents:

THE BATES FAMILY
"Sausage and Beer," 1
"Small Point Bridge," 13
"Windy Fourth," 24
"The Tide and Isaac Bates," 39
ILLUSIONS/DREAMS
"Grubbing for Roots," 52
"Bruno in the Hall of Mirrors," 68
"Greek Mysteries," 84
"I Remember the Day God Died Like It Was Yesterday," 100
GENERATIONS
"Crossings," 111
"Teddy, Where Are You?" 121
"Mars Revisited," 135
"Estuaries," 151

A Season for Unnatural Causes, Philip F. O'Connor

Contents:

Curving Road, John Stewart

Contents:

Such Waltzing Was Not Easy, Gordon Weaver

Contents:

"When Times Sit In," 114
"Kiss in the Hand," 125

1976

Rolling All the Time, James Ballard

Contents:

"Introductory Aeronautics," 1
"Wild Honey," 26
"The Feast of Crispian," 40
"Down by the Riverside," 92
"Rolling All the Time," 110
"In the City," 146
"Hundred to One," 159

Love in the Winter, Daniel Curley

Contents:

"Love in the Winter," 1
"Who, What, When, Where—Why?" 16
"The Great Day," 26
"Why I Play Rugby," 41
"In Northumberland Once," 51
"A View of the Mountains," 73
"Perhaps Love," 79
"The Eclipse," 90
"Power Line," 98
"What Rough Beast?" 109

To Byzantium, Andrew Fetler

Contents:

"To Byzantium," 1
"The Pillow from Niagara Falls," 15
"The Mandolin," 27
"The Mozart Lover," 32
"Demons," 52
"Longface," 69

Small Moments, Nancy Huddleston Packer

Contents:

1977

One More River, Lester Goldberg

Contents:

The Tennis Player and Other Stories, Kent Nelson

Contents:

A Horse of Another Color, Carolyn Osborn

Contents:

The Pleasures of Manhood, Robley Wilson, Jr.

Contents:

1978
The New World Tales, Russell Banks

Contents:

Part I: Renunciation
"The Custodian," 3
"The Perfect Couple," 9
"A Sentimental Education," 23
"About the Late Zimma (Penny) Cate: Selections from Her Loving
   Husband's Memory Hoard," 31
"The Conversion," 37
Part II: Transformation
"The Rise of the Middle Class," 83
"Indisposed," 88
"The Caul," 97
"The Adjutant Bird," 105
"The New World," 111

The Actes and Monuments, John William Corrington

Contents:

"The Actes and Monuments," 1
"Old Men Dream Dreams, Young Men See Visions," 36
"Pleadings," 46
"Keep Them Cards and Letters Comin' In," 85
"Every Act Whatever of Man," 99

Virginia Reels, William Hoffman

Contents:

"The Spirit in Me," 1
"Sea Tides," 15
"The Darkened Room," 32
"Your Hand, Your Hand," 45
"Amazing Grace," 61
"A Darkness on the Mountain," 81
"A Southern Sojourn," 98

"A Walk by the River," 112
"Sea Treader," 126

Up Where I Used to Live, Max Schott

Contents:

"Up Where I Used to Live," 1
"Sterling's Calf," 22
"Early Winter," 27
"The Old Flame," 57
"The Horsebreaker," 73
"The Drowning," 90
"The Sinner," 101
"Eulogy," 117
"Brotherly Love," 134

1979

The Return of Service, Jonathan Baumbach

Contents:

"The Traditional Story Returns," 1
"Another Look at the Blackbird," 9
"Neglected Masterpieces IV," 28
"The Adventures of King Dong," 36
"The Fields of Obscurity," 48
"A Moving Story," 60
"Crossed in Love by Her Eyes," 71
"Birthday Gifts," 84
"The Curse," 95
"Disguises," 106
"The Penthouse Heist," 114
"The Return of Service," 126

On the Edge of the Desert, Gladys Swan

Contents:

"Losing Game," 1
"Decline and Fall," 17
"Ghosts," 35

Surviving Adverse Seasons, Barry Targan

Contents:

The Gasoline Wars, Jean Thompson

Contents:

1980

Desirable Aliens, John Bovey

Contents:

Naming Things, H. E. Francis

Contents:

Transports and Disgraces, Robert Henson

Contents:

The Calling, Mary Gray Hughes

Contents:

ies Who Knit for a Living, Anthony E. Stockanes

tents:

982
astorale, Susan Engberg

Contents:

Home Fires, David Long

Contents:

1981

***Into the Wind*, Robert Henderson**

Contents:

***Breaking and Entering*, Peter Makuck**

Contents:

***The Four Corners of the House*, Abraham Rothber**

Contents:

The Canyons of Grace, Levi S. Peterson

Contents:

Barbara, B. Wongar

Contents:

1983

No books issued in the series.

1984

Bodies of the Rich, John J. Clayton

Contents:

"Cambridge Is Sinking!" 44
"Part-time Father," 64
"Prewar Quality," 80
"Fantasy for a Friday Afternoon," 96
"Bodies of the Rich," 113

Music Lesson, Martha Lacy Hall

Contents:

"Privacy," 1
"Music Lesson," 12
"The Painter," 19
"Lucky Life," 30
"Doll," 39
"Joanna," 50
"Just a Little Sore Throat," 65
"The Visit," 77
"The Peaceful Eye," 99
"The Man Who Gave Brother Double Pneumonia," 112

Fetching the Dead, Scott R. Sanders

Contents:

"The Recovery of Vision," 1
"Fetching the Dead," 18
"Wake," 37
"Walking to Sleep," 56
"The Cry," 77
"Prophet," 96
"The Fire Woman," 111
"Time and Again," 127

Some of the Things I Did Not Do, Janet Beeler Shaw

Contents:

"Love and Other Lessons," 1
"The Cat Who Fought the Rain," 13
"The Geese at Presque Isle," 25
"In High Country," 39
"The Courtship of the Thin Girl," 52

"Saturday Night in Pinedale, Wyoming," 64
"The Trail to the Ledge," 77
"A New Life," 90
"Inventing the Kiss," 106
"Some of the Things I Did Not Do," 119

1985

Honeymoon, Merrill Joan Gerber

Contents:

"Honeymoon," 1
"At the Fence," 16
"Straight from the Deathbed," 30
"Tragic Lives," 42
"Someone Should Know This Story," 55
"The Mistress of Goldman's Antiques," 66
"Memorial Service," 82
"I Don't Believe This," 97
"Witnesses," 108

Tentacles of Unreason, Joan Givner

Contents:

"First Love," 1
"Brains," 17
"A Spectator Sport," 32
"The Testament of Leyla," 51
"The Lost Sheep," 60
"A Climate of Extremes," 70
"Laocoön, My Father," 82
"Conversation Pieces," 91
"The Celebrant," 108
"The Decline and Fall of a Reasonable Woman," 121

The Christmas Wife, Helen Norris

Contents:

"The Love Child," 1
"The Quarry," 17
"The Christmas Wife," 31

Getting to Know the Weather, Pamela Painter

Contents:

Birds Landing, Ernest J. Finney

Contents:

1986
Serious Trouble, Paul Friedman

Contents:

Tigers in the Wood, Rebecca Kavaler

Contents:

The Greek Generals Talk: Memoires of the Trojan War, Phillip Parotti

Contents:

1987

Singing on the Titanic, Perry Glasser

Contents:

Legacies, Nancy Potter

Contents:

Beyond This Bitter Air, Sarah Rossiter

Contents:

Scenes from the Homefront, Sara Vogan

Contents:

"Scenes from the Homefront," 1
"No Other Women," 20
"Miss Buick of 1942," 32
"The Crane Wife," 46
"Angels in the Snow," 58
"The Confession of the Finch," 71
"The Strength of Steel," 80
"Sunday's No Name Band," 95
"China across the Bay," 101
"Mozart in the Afternoon," 117
"Hearts of a Shark," 124

1988
Tumbling, Kermit Moyer

Contents:

"In the Castle," 1
"Tumbling," 10
"Life Jackets," 39
"The Compass of the Heart," 52
"Coming Unbalanced," 73
"Movements of the Hand," 91
"Ruth's Daughter," 103

Water into Wine, Helen Norris

Contents:

"The Cororant," 1
"Mrs. Moonlight," 24
"The Light on the Water," 41
"White Hyacinths," 60
"The Cloven Tree," 92
"The Pearl Sitter," 118
"Water into Wine," 137

The Trojan Generals Talk: Memoires of the Greek War,
Phillip Parotti

Contents:

Playing with Shadows, Gloria Whelan

Contents:

Prime Number: 17 Stories from Illinois Short Fiction, ed. Ann Lowry Weir, introduction by George C. Core

Contents:

"The Actes and Monuments," John William Corrington, 32
"Pastorale," Susan Engberg, 67
"At the Fence," Merrill Joan Gerber, 86
"One More River," Lester Goldberg, 100
"Billie Loses Her Job," Robert Henson, 113
"Home Fires," David Long, 140
"The Christmas Wife, Helen Norris, 154
"Early Morning, Lonely Ride," Nancy Huddleston Packer, 174
"The Next Time I Meet Buddy Rich," Pamela Painter, 187
"The Red Dress," Abraham Rothberg, 199
"A New Life," Janet Beeler Shaw, 216
"Ladies Who Knit for a Living," Anthony E. Stockanes, 232
"Surviving Adverse Seasons," Barry Targan, 258
"Birds in Air," Jean Thompson, 303
"The Two Sides of Things," Gordon Weaver, 312

1989
Man Without Memory, Richard Burgin

Contents:

"Notes on Mrs. Slaughter," 1
"Constitution Day," 14
"New City," 30
"The Opposite Girl," 40
"Mason," 50
"Man without Memory," 64
"Aerialist," 79
"Carlin's Trio," 92
"The Victims," 106

The People Down South, Cary C. Holladay

Contents:

"Keepers," 1
"The People Down South," 11
"County of Rage, County of Young Green Growing Things," 25
"To Ashes," 32
"Squabs," 39
"Smoketown Road," 44
"A Neighborhood Story," 51

Bodies at Sea, Erin McGraw

Contents:

Falling Free, Barry Targan

Contents:

1990

No books issued in the series. Publication was resumed in 1991.

AUTHOR INDEX

Bovey, John. *Desirable Aliens*. 1980.
Burgin, Richard. *Man Without Memory*. 1989.

Clayton, John J. *Bodies of the Rich*. 1984.
Corrington, John William. *The Actes and Monuments*. 1978.
Curley, Daniel. *Love in the Winter*. 1976.

Engberg, Susan. *Pastorale*. 1982.

Fetler, Andrew. *To Byzantium*. 1976.
Finney, Ernest. *Birds Landing*. 1986.
Francis, H.E. *Naming Things*. 1980.
Friedman, Paul. *Serious Trouble*. 1986.

Gerber, Joan Merrill. *Honeymoon*. 1985.
Givner, Joan. *Tentacles of Unreason*. 1985.
Glasser, Perry. *Singing on the Titanic*. 1987.
Goldberg, Lester. *One More River*. 1977.

Hall, Martha Lacy. *Music Lessons*. 1984.
Henderson, Robert. *Into the Wind*. 1980.
Henson, Robert. *Transports and Disgraces*. 1980.
Hoffman, William. *Virginia Reels*. 1978.
Holladay, Cary C. *The People Down South*. 1989.
Hughes, Mary Gray. *The Calling*. 1980.

Kavaler, Rebecca. *Tigers in the Wood*. 1986.

Long, David. *Home Fires*. 1982.

Makuck, Peter. *Breaking and Entering*. 1980.
McGraw, Erin. *Bodies at Sea*. 1989.
Minot, Stephen. *Crossings*. 1975.
Moyer, Kermit. *Tumbling*. 1988.

Nelson, Kent. *The Tennis Player*. 1977.
Norris, Helen. *The Christmas Wife*. 1985.
———. *Water into Wine*. 1988.

O'Connor, Philip F. *A Season for Unnatural Causes*. 1975.
Osborn, Carolyn. *A Horse of Another Color*. 1977.

TITLE INDEX (BY COLLECTION)

Calling, The, Mary Gray Hughes. 1980.
Canyons of Grace, The, Levi Peterson. 1982.
Christmas Wife, The, Helen Norris. 1985.
Crossings, Stephen Minot. 1975.
Curving Road, John Stewart. 1975.

Desirable Aliens, John Bovey. 1980.

Falling Free, Barry Targan. 1989.
Fetching the Dead, Scott R. Sanders. 1984.
Four Corners of the House, The, Abraham Rothberg. 1980.

Gasoline Wars, The, Jean Thompson. 1979.
Getting to Know the Weather, Pamela Painter. 1985.
Greek Generals Talk, The, Phillip Parotti. 1986.

Home Fires, David Long. 1982.
Honeymoon, Merrill Joan Gerber. 1985.
Horse of Another Color, A, Carolyn Osborn. 1977.

Into the Wind, Robert Henderson. 1980.

Ladies Who Knit for a Living, Anthony E. Stockanes. 1980.
Legacies, Nancy Potter. 1987.
Love in the Winter, Daniel Curley. 1976.

Man Without Memory, Richard Burgin. 1989.
Music Lesson, Martha Lacy Hall. 1984.

Naming Things, H. E. Francis. 1980.
New World, The, Russell Banks. 1978.

One More River, Lester Goldberg. 1977.
On the Edge of the Desert, Gladys Swan. 1979.

Pastorale, Susan Engberg. 1982.
People Down South, The, Cary C. Holladay. 1989.
Playing with Shadows, Gloria Whelan. 1988.
Pleasures of Manhood, The. Robley Wilson, Jr. 1977.
Prime Number: 17 Stories from Illinois Short Fiction, ed. Ann
      Lowry Weir. 1988.

Return of Service, The, Jonathan Baumbach. 1979.
Rolling All the Time, James Ballard. 1976.

Scenes from the Homefront, Sara Vogan. 1987.
Season of Unnatural Causes, A, Philip F. O'Connor. 1975.
Serious Trouble, Paul Friedman. 1986.
Singing on the Titanic, Perry Glasser. 1987.
Small Moments, Nancy Huddleston Packer. 1976.
Some of the Things I Did Not Do, Janet Beeler Shaw. 1984.
Such Waltzing Was Not Easy, Gordon Weaver. 1975.
Surviving Adverse Seasons, Barry Targan. 1979.

Tennis Player, The, Kent Nelson. 1977.
Tentacles of Unreason, Joan Givner. 1985.
Tigers in the Wood, Rebecca Kavaler. 1986.
To Byzantium, Andrew Fetler. 1976.
Transports and Disgraces, Robert Henson. 1980.
Trojan Generals Talk, The, Phillip Parotti. 1988.
Tumbling, Kermit Moyer. 1988.

Up Where I Used to Live, Max Schott. 1978.

Virginia Reels, William Hoffman. 1978.

Water into Wine, Helen Norris, 1988.

Iowa School of Letters Award, 1970–90

As the Iowa School of Letters, at the University of Iowa, Iowa City, was the first American university creative writing program, developed more than fifty years ago, it seems fitting that the Iowa School of Letters Award, first given in 1970, is the oldest of the short fiction award series presented here. Tailored for new authors, the award is open to any writer who has not previously published a volume of prose fiction. The fact that the writers have not yet published a volume of fiction, however, does not mean that their work is anything less than professional, highly polished, and accomplished. A refreshing aspect of this competition is that, like the Drue Heinz and Pushcart prizes, the writer is not required to pay an entry fee.

In recent years, two awards have been presented annually—the Iowa Short Fiction Award and the John Simmons Short Fiction Award; only the former is included here since the latter is very new.

An individual judge evaluates each work. Judges have included John Hawkes, William Gass, Joyce Carol Oates, George Garrett, Stanley Elkin, John Gardner, Doris Grumbach, Raymond Carver, Frederick Busch, Tim O'Brien, Tobias Wolff, Alison Lurie, Robert Stone, and Gail Godwin.

Winners of the Iowa School of Letters Award, all volumes published by University of Iowa Press, Iowa City, IA 52240.

1972: *The Burning & Other Stories*, Jack Cady

Contents:

1973: *The Itinerary of Beggars*, H. E. Francis

Contents:

"Where Was My Life Before I Died?" 229
"Contemplations of Ecstasy on the Day of My Suicide," 246
"Running," 263

1974: *After the First Death There Is No Other*, Natalie L. M. Petesch

Contents:

"The Grievance Adjuster," 1
"A Brief Biography of Ellie Brume," 20
"My Crystal," 29
"John Stuart Mill Goes Home," 39
"Ramón El Conejo," 49
"L'il Britches," 65
"Nails," 72
"Stones," 84
"Selma," 93
"The Playhouse," 108
"The Girl Who Was Afraid of Snow," 122
"How I Saved Mickey From the Bomb," 136
"The End of the World," 155
"Bye Bye Birdie," 163
"The Festival," 184

1975: *Harry Belten and the Mendelssohn Violin Concerto*, Barry Targan

Contents:

"Harry Belten and the Mendelssohn Violin Concerto," 1
"Little Parameters," 32
"Old Vemish," 53
"The Man Who Lived," 96
"Leave My Mother Alone," 111
"Natural As Can Be," 125
"The Clay War," 135
"Charity Begins," 161
"Leaving," 183
"*In Excelsis Deo*," 196

"And Their Fathers Who Begat Them," 204
"Tickets," 228
"Elizabeth Lanier," 243
". . . . And Still the Heart Doth Sing," 259

1976: *The Black Velvet Girl*, C. E. Poverman

Contents:

"Deathmasks of Xo," 1
"The Electric Dress," 19
"Retour Du Sahara," 41
"Big Blues," 76
"Jade," 97
"In the Remains of Her Speech," 110
"Every Man Should Have an Asian Wife," 131
"Resurrection at Hanauma Bay," 165
"Sports Illustrated," 182
"The Gift: Bihar, India," 193
"Tooth," 211
"A Short Apocryphal Tale of the Sea My Father Would Deny
    Anyway," 229
"The Black Velvet Girl," 238

1977: *The Women in the Mirror*, Pat Carr

Contents:

"The Party," 1
"Miss Amelia's," 9
"Sunday Morning," 19
"Progress Report—Candelaria Project," 24
"The Peeping Tom," 34
"Mermaids Singing," 41
"Exiles," 48
"Pascuas Caleñas," 54
"Indian Burial," 61
"The Cake-Eaters," 68
"Bullfight," 75
"Wrought Iron Lace," 81
"A Visit from the Consul," 89
"October Afternoon Conference," 98

"Mrs. Jessie Martha Jones," 103
"An Evening's Seduction," 108
"The Witch of Peach Tree Street," 113
"Rite of Passage," 121
"Andrew's Mistress," 128
"Incident at Finnegan's Wake," 134

1978: *A Nest of Hooks*, Lon Otto

Contents:

"The Story," 1
"With Horse People," 2
"Her Hair," 6
"Terror," 9
"The Rules," 18
"Submarine Warfare on the Upper Mississippi," 19
"Tact," 23
"The Gardener's Story," 24
"Three Places," 27
"Love Poems," 33
"Bread Murder," 34
"I'm Sorry That You're Dead," 36
"Entry," 44
"Waiting for the Freedom Train," 45
"The Milwaukee Poets," 49
"Cello," 52
"The Bicycle That Went Mad," 53
"A Regular Old Time Miser," 58
"The Wish-Fulfillment Camera," 60
"Background Music," 69
"The Labors of Love," 71
"A Very Short Story," 77
"A Nest of Hooks," 78
"What Happened to Bill Day?" 80
"The Cruelty of Dreams," 91
"Welfare Island," 92
"A Good Year for Them," 101
"The Siege," 102

1979: *Fly Away Home*, Mary Hedin

Contents:

1980: *Impossible Appetites*, James Fetler

Contents:

1981: *The Phototropic Woman*, Annabel Thomas

Contents:

1982: *Shiny Objects*, Dianne Benedict

Contents:

1983: *Heart Failure*, Ivy Goodman

Contents:

"Revenge," 97
"Heart Failure," 105
"Telephones," 113
"Pinecone," 119
"Resignation," 127

1984: *Old Wives' Tales*, Susan M. Dodd

Contents:

"Rue," 1
"Coelostat," 25
"Public Appearances," 43
"Wild Men of Borneo," 63
"One Hundred Years of Solicitude: The Meditations of Ursula," 75
"Walls," 89
"Potions," 109
"Snowbird," 123
"Berkie," 145
"Browsing," 171

1985: *Dancing in the Movies*, Robert Boswell

Contents:

"Little Bear," 1
"Kentucky," 25
"Dancing in the Movies," 39
"The Darkness of Love," 63
"Flipflops," 111
"The Right Thing," 125

1986: *Eminent Domain*, Dan O'Brien (Co-Winner)

Contents:

"Winter Cat," 1
"Cowboy on the Concord Bridge," 17
"Seals," 27
"Eminent Domain," 41
"The Inheritance," 53

"Weightless," 79
"The Wild Geese," 93
"Strand of Wire," 103
"Final Touches," 111
"The Georgia Breeze," 125

1986: *Resurrectionists*, Russell Working (Co-winner)

Contents:

"Charis," 1
"Resurrectionists," 23
"Shooting," 53
"Rendering Byzantium," 61
"Pictures of her Snake," 107
"The Monkey," 115
"Famous People," 137
"On Freedom," 149

1987: *Fruit of the Month*, Abby Frucht (Co-winner)

Contents:

"Midnight," 1
"Peace and Passivity," 17
"Fruit of the Month," 33
"Engagements," 47
"Paradise," 63
"The Anniversary," 73
"Winter," 83
"How to Live Alone," 93
"Trees at Night," 107
"Fate and the Poet," 119
"Nuns in Love," 137
"The Habit of Friendship," 151

1987: *Star Game*, Lucia Nevai (Co-winner)

Contents:

"Temp," 1
"Mother's Day," 9
"The Nile," 21

"Connor's Lake," 33
"Star Game," 41
"Stranger in Paradise," 51
"The Sad-Womb Son," 67
"Likely Houses," 73
"Diamond Twill," 85
"Baby Wood," 97
"Mr. Feathers," 109
"Resident Artist," 123
"Hooked," 131
"Red Spikes," 139

1988: *The Long White*, Sharon Dilworth

Contents:

"Winter Mines," 1
"Mad Dog Queen," 17
"Miles from Coconut Grove," 37
"The Seeney Stretch," 57
"Lunching at Archibald's," 73
"The Lady on the Plane," 89
"Independence Day," 107
"Lip Service Résumé," 119
"The Long White," 141

1989: *Lent: The Slow Fast*, Starkey Flythe, Jr.

Contents:

"Lent: The Slow Fast," 1
"The Ice Fisher," 13
"For a Good Time Call Matthew," 25
"CVIO," 37
"The Coalition," 49
"Every Known Diversion," 67
"Learning Italian," 85
"Walking, Walking," 95
"The Water Cure," 111
"The Glass of Milk," 129
"Point of Conversion," 139

1990: *A Hole in the Language*, Marly Swick

Contents:

"Elba," 1
"Heart," 23
"The Rhythm of Disintegration," 41
"Eating Alone," 59
"Camelot," 79
"The Zealous Mourner," 101
"A Hole in the Language," 125
"Movie Music," 149
"Monogamy," 169

1990: ***Traps***, Sondra Spatt Olsen

Contents:

"The Butcher's Girl," 1
"Harmony," 11
"Working Nights as a Pickle," 21
"Topaze," 31
"44–28," 43
"To Forget August," 51
"A Rent-Stabilized Romance," 59
"Surfaces," 67
"Gypsy Ways," 77
"Who Could Love a Fat Man?" 93
"Quintessence of Zoe," 107
"An Old-fashioned Woman," 121
"Free Writing," 131

Fetler, James. *Impossible Appetites*. 1980.
Flythe, Starkey, Jr. *Lent: The Slow Fast*. 1989.
Francis, H. E. *The Itinerary of Beggars*. 1973.
Frucht, Abby. *Fruit of the Month*. Co-winner 1987.

Goodman, Ivy. *Heart Failure*. 1983.

Hedin, Mary. *Fly Away Home*. 1979.

Neval, Lucia. *Star Game*. Co-winner 1987.

O'Brien, Dan. *Eminent Domain*. Co-winner 1986.
O'Connor, Philip F. *Old Morals, Small Continents, Darker Times*. 1971.
Olsen, Sondra Spatt. *Traps*. 1990.
Otto, Lon. *A Nest of Hooks*. 1978.

Petesch, Natalie. *After the First Death There Is No Other*. 1974.
Poverman, C.E. *The Black Velvet Girl*. 1976.

Swick, Marly. *A Hole in the Language*. 1990.

Targan, Barry. *Harry Belten and the Mendelssohn Violin Concerto*. 1975.
Thomas, Annabel. *The Phototropic Woman*. 1981.

Working, Russell. *Resurrectionists*. Co-winner 1986.

TITLE INDEX (BY COLLECTION)

Fruit of the Month, Abby Frucht. Co-winner 1987.

Harry Belten and the Mendelssohn Violin Concerto, Barry Targan. 1975.
Heart Failure, Ivy Goodman. 1983.
Hole in the Language, A, Marly Swick. 1990.

Impossible Appetites, James Fetler. 1980.
Itinerary of Beggars, The, H. E. Francis. 1973.

Lent: The Slow Fast, Starkey Flythe, Jr. 1989.
Long White, The, Sharon Dilworth. 1988.

Nest of Hooks, A, Lon Otto. 1978.

Old Morals, Small Continents, Darker Times, Philip F. O'Connor. 1971.
Old Wives' Tales, Susan M. Dodd. 1984.

Phototropic Woman, The, Annabel Thomas. 1981.

Resurrectionists, Russell Working. Co-winner 1986.
Shiny Objects, Dianne Benedict. 1982.
Star Game, Lucia Neval. Co-winner 1987.

Traps, Sondra Spatt Olsen. 1990.

Women in the Mirror, The, Pat Carr. 1977.